# APPLES
*A Cookbook*

# APPLES
## A Cookbook

CHARTWELL
BOOKS, INC.

# A QUANTUM BOOK

Published by Chartwell Books
A Division of Book Sales Inc
114 Northfield Avenue
Edison, New Jersey 08837
USA

ISBN 0-7858-0790-X

QUMABK

This book was produced by
Quantum Books Ltd
6 Blundell Street
London N7 9BH

Printed in Singapore by Star Standard Industries Pte Ltd

## A C K N O W L E D G M E N T S

I would especially like to thank Caroline Hirsch, Jamie Beecroft, Rita Barol, Jimmy Stanton and all my friends and family at Delta 88 Restaurant and Caroline's at the Seaport for all their love and encouragement, not just on this project but in all my endeavors.

Thanks to Michelle Hauser. Thanks to Sam and Nancy Freitag, William and Mildred Raucher and Loretta and Bruno Hauser. Thanks to all my good friends.

Thanks also to Marta Hallett, Ellen Milionis, Linda Greet, Lindsey Crittenden and Ellie Watson and all the support at Running Heads, as well as to Caroline Herter, Rebecca Verrill and Sydny Miner at Simon & Schuster.

We would like to thank the following people for their support during this project: the Jacobson and Ehlers families, Judy Devine for her inspiration and love, Dexter Samuel for his great energy and smiles while assisting with the photography, Maggie Jones and Leontine Klein for loaning their wonderful props, and Gary Larson for filling the studio with laughter. Thanks also to Jill Bock, Greg Corso, Beth Farb, Simon Feldman, Robbin Gourley, Kim Kelling, Joey Quintal, Jeffrey Stern, Barbara Vitanza and Myriam Zwierzinska.

Our special thanks to those companies who generously loaned us their beautiful wares: Country Floors, Dean & DeLuca, Fitz and Floyd, Platypus, Jeffrey Weiss New York, and especially Douglas Weiss at Pottery Barn and Pauline Kelly at Zona.

Wilted Greens with
Red Delicious Apples and Bacon
42

Cracked Wheat Salad with
Jonathan Apples and Mint
44

Smoked Turkey and
Gravenstein Apple Salad
46

Rome Apple and
Goat Cheese Tartlets
48

Greening Apple
and Spinach Pâté
50

# THREE
## MAIN COURSES

Baked Cortland Apples
with Yam Filling
54

Grilled Swordfish with
Lady Apple Butter
56

Brook Trout Baked in Parchment with
Northern Spy Apples
58

Barbecued Shrimp with
Jonathan Apple and Quince Chutney
60

Red Snapper with
Empire Apples and Walnuts
62

Turkey Potpie with
Newtown Pippins and Onions
64

Duck Breasts with Crab Apples
66

Chicken and
Cortland Apple Couscous
68

Pork Chops with Rome Apple
and Rosemary Stuffing
70

## SIX
### BEVERAGES

### RECIPE LIST

### RECIPE LIST BY APPLE OR APPLE PRODUCT

# INTRODUCTION

Versatile, enduring, delicate – these qualities describe the apple as a concept as well as a food. The apple is as much a part of the iconography of cooking and folk culture as a stove, a pot or a ladle; so much so that the mere mention of, say, apple pie is often enough to evoke images and memories that are inextricably associated with the pie: a picnic, a birthday, a family holiday gathering.

When I thought of doing my next cookbook these associations immediately suggested a collection of traditional recipes, but with a slight twist: recipes from different traditions, like Southern American, Slavic and British among others. Several factors contribute to the making of a traditional cuisine: regional ingredients, economic conditions and their effect on cooking and storage facilities and, sometimes, religious restrictions. Another contributing factor is the passage of time. The nuances of a dish can vary from one occasion to the next or from one generation to the next. This is natural.

But what makes a dish traditional is if its form remains constant through its many executions. In fact many cultures share similar forms for their national dishes, and only vary in their ingredients. Consider, for example, the similarities between a tortilla and a pita, a ravioli and a pierogi, or a blintz and a crêpe. As an American chef what draws me to the kitchen is the pursuit of the roots and development of American dishes. The melting-pot principle that so sharply affects so much of our culture is most evident in our cooking. Coleslaw, hamburgers, omelets – these dishes are Scandinavian, English and French in origin. How these dishes became adapted to American culture goes beyond the old story of settlers from these countries bringing their national foods with them. An unusual evolution occurs when somebody attempts a dish not native to their culture. They attach their own innate sensibilities and come up with something slightly different. It is an issue of assimilation, like the way an immigrant named Sven becomes Steven, or Johannes becomes John. The old and new characteristics merge and form a new landscape of language, arts and food.

The apple is a natural representative of American cooking and culture. It is a common ingredient throughout most of the world's cooking, so international dishes appear to be right at home. It is an ingredient that can be manipulated in many ways, maintain its identity and still yield itself to its intended use. It can be sautéed, baked, fried, grilled or just sliced. It works wonderfully with meats, in salads, in desserts or by itself. An apple is a fruit that has a thin but tough skin, a very tough core, inedible seeds, and firm, fibrous meat that accounts for about 90 percent of its composition. Depending on the variety, apples can be sweet, juicy, tart, sour, even salty. As a cooking ingredient the apple usually does what you tell it to do. However, there are a few basic principles to keep in mind.

The skin is a valuable ingredient, containing what many consider to be the essence of the apple's flavor, but it is useful in some recipes and obtrusive in others. The skin of an apple has a high concentration of fructose (natural fruit sugar) and a substance called pectin, which provides a gelatinous, thickening element to recipes such as jams or jellies. (Pectin can be extracted from apple skins, and is sold commercially in powder form.) In a recipe for applesauce or apple butter (such as Ginger Crab Apple Applesauce) where the pectin and fructose contribute highly to the final outcome of the dish, the skin can be cooked along with the meat and core and seeds (which also contain smaller amounts of fructose and pectin) to great advantage. After they have given off all they can give, the entire fruit can be forced through a sieve so just the meat is used and the skin, seeds and core are discarded.

Because of the dense, fibrous nature of the meat of the apple, the type of heat or cooking technique used will affect these fibers in different ways. As when cooking any dish, when I cook with apples I try to work backwards. I think of how I want the dish to taste, and from that I can derive what ingredients to use and how to go about preparing them. Try putting an apple through various cooking procedures to learn how to elicit the results that you want in your dishes. First cut the apple into quarters, then peel the skin off and cut a little scoop in the center to remove the seeds.

If you take these apple quarters and drop them into hot oil, the outer fibers will react to the sudden extreme heat by tightening up and forming a crust. The oil itself won't penetrate these tightened outer fibers, but the heat from the oil will cook the apple through. When the apple is eaten it will maintain its shape on the outside, but will be tender on the inside. Apples cooked in this way make a balanced accompaniment to a salad, mimicking the crispness of the greens and providing a contrast in texture as well as in temperature, as in the recipe for Smoked Turkey and Gravenstein Apple Salad.

Cut the quarters into smaller chunks and sauté them in a little butter and an altogether different effect is achieved. The outside is not as crispy as the fried pieces and the inside is not as tender because the temperature of the butter is lower than that of the oil. Instead the apple is uniformly soft but not mushy. This is a fine complement to a food of an even softer texture, such as baked fillet of fish, where the apple provides a texture ever so slightly firmer than the seafood. Add some toasted nuts to the apples and fish and there are now three interesting levels of texture, as in Red Snapper with Empire Apples and Walnuts.

Place the apple chunks in cold water or fruit juice, bring the liquid to a boil, then lower to a simmer, and the fibers of the apple soften and separate evenly. The fibers that hold the apple together eventually break down completely and become applesauce.

The art of cooking with apples is not limited to the handling of their fibrous nature; it also lies in knowing how the many cooking procedures affect the flavors that are found so intensely in apples, and how these flavors and textures all interact within the context of the dish. Sometimes I add a little salt or lemonjuice to apples at various stages of their preparation. This does several things. Salt especially helps to activate certain sugars within the apple (as it does in Macoun Apple Pie) and can accelerate cooking, while lemon juice helps to retard cooking. Salt or lemon juice, combined with those sugars, confuse the palate so it's not sure what it's tasting. This trickery is what keeps some eating experiences lively and entertaining. There are other ways to achieve the same effect, such as combining apples with onions, potatoes or any number of herbs and spices; serving apples with fish or pork or veal; or making an apple-based soup.

Cooking with apples can also mean making use of the many valuable apple products that should be a staple in every kitchen. These include several types of cider which all offer their own different identities: There are alcoholic or "hard" ciders as well as many nonalcoholic varieties ranging from freshly pressed autumn cider to bottled sparkling cider. When fermented, cider makes a full-flavored vinegar. All of these can be used to create sauces, marinades and salad dressings. Calvados is a fine brandy made from cider and similar to cognac or Armagnac; it can also be used in marinades and sauces, to perfume cakes, or in Calvados Soufflé. Warm cider with a splash of calvados is a welcome comfort on a cold day, or on a hot day a Calvados Spritzer can be quite refreshing. Applejack is a less refined cousin of calvados; the two make suitable substitutes for each other in recipes. Dried apples are another great apple product to cook with. They have little moisture and so are able to withstand most cooking processes without losing their shape or concentrated flavor, and can be a wonderfully chewy addition to baked goods such as Apple-Hazelnut Muffins. All these ingredients can contribute to making delicious, uncommon meals.

Another of the exciting things about cooking with apples is the lavish variety of apples. There are over 7,500 types of apples grown throughout the world; 2,500 are available in the United States alone. The most common apple in the American market is the Red Delicious. Stately, beautiful and dark red, it is what many most readily visualize when thinking of apples. Its success is not based on its flavor, which is really quite bland, as much as its ability to ship and store well. There are also Golden Delicious, which are roundish and rich yellow with little black freckles. The Golden Delicious has a sweet, juicy flavor, and is excellent for salads because of its resistance to browning. There is the Granny Smith, increasing in popularity, a bright green apple with an extremely firm texture and a tart, dry flavor. When the Granny Smith is cooked, the tartness is mellowed but the texture tends to dry a little, easily remedied by adding sugar to such recipes as apple pie. The Rome (or Rome Beauty) is large and deep red, almost perfectly round. It is primarily a cooking apple, with less flavor when eaten raw. But when baked, a richly mellow, almost savory flavor emerges. The Northern Spy is large and pale yellow-green with thin pink stripes coming out of the center. It is a beautiful apple with a gentle, tart flavor. It is a great apple for salads or for sautéing. One of my favorite farmer's market discoveries is the Winesap. This apple has a dense red skin with black-and-white freckles and very firm, white meat. It is most succulent and juicy, almost wine-flavored. I have to buy more than I need because I can't resist them and eventually eat some before I reach my kitchen.

Who is to say which apples do best for which dishes? I have been told, and have read, not to cook with Granny Smiths, just to eat them raw. But I have made delicious apple pies with thinly sliced Granny Smiths, a little sugar and a pinch of salt. I have heard not to bake MacIntoshes, but they seem perfect in apple cobblers. While it is true that there are some apples that do better than others in some situations, only through experimentation can you determine which can successfully substitute for others in any given recipe.

The following general guidelines should help in deciding which apples to try substituting for others, but don't be afraid to experiment with apples outside of these categories. Of the apples used in this book, Cortlands, Empires, Granny Smiths, Gravensteins, Jonathans, Lady apples, Macouns, MacIntoshes, Newtown Pippins and Northern Spies are all considered all-purpose apples, suitable for cooking or eating raw. Within this group, some are often better than others for certain applications:

Cortlands, as in Baked Cortland Apples with Yam Filling, are great for baking whole (especially in the microwave) because they maintain their shape; Jonathans and MacIntoshes can be a good choice for quick-cooking methods or for applesauce or soup, like MacIntosh Apple and Blue Cheese Bisque, because they tend to lose their shape; and the Northern Spy's flavor develops well when cooked, but Gravensteins taste better raw. Only two of the apples used in this book are generally regarded as best eaten raw: the Red and Golden Delicious. Three are most often cooked before eating: Crab Apples, Greenings and Romes. One other factor to keep in mind when looking for an apple substitute is flavor: tart substitutes for tart, sweet for sweet, and so on. For instance Greenings and Granny Smiths, both very tart, could replace each other in a recipe; Macouns and MacIntoshes, which are relatives, are very similar in taste; and Winesaps might be suitable stand-ins for Jonathans as they both have a savory flavor.

The only rule is that there are no rules. Once you are familiar with the different varieties of apples and apple products and their properties, you will be able to elicit the response you want and achieve your culinary goals.

# ONE
## BREAKFAST
## AND BRUNCH

# OAT GRIDDLE CAKES WITH JONATHAN APPLES AND PECANS

1¹/₂ cups oatmeal

1¹/₂ cups boiling water

1 egg

1 cup flour

2 tablespoons baking powder

pinch of salt

¹/₄ cup sugar

1 cup milk

¹/₄ cup melted butter

3 Jonathan apples, peeled, cored and chopped

¹/₂ cup pecan pieces

2 tablespoons butter

Makes about 15 3-inch pancakes

Preparation time: 45 minutes

Combine oatmeal and boiling water. Let stand 5 minutes.

Add egg, flour, baking powder, salt and sugar. Mix.

Stir in milk, melted butter, apples and pecans.

Melt 2 tablespoons butter in a large, flat skillet or griddle over medium heat.

When the butter begins to crackle, spoon on pancake batter to desired size. Gently flip pancakes when bubbles form around the edges and in the center. Cook for another minute and serve with maple syrup.

# ROME APPLE, ORANGE AND PRUNE COMPOTE

1 orange

¹/₄ cup sugar (or less to taste)

6 pitted prunes

1 Rome apple, peeled, cored and diced

2 ounces dark rum or cognac

Peel orange and cut into sections, carefully removing membranes and white pith. Cut peel into thin strips.

In a heavy skillet, dissolve sugar in 1 cup water. Boil for 4 to 5 minutes. Add orange peel and prunes. Continue boiling for another 4 to 5 minutes.

Lower heat to a simmer. Add apple and orange sections. Cook until apple is tender, adding more water if necessary. Remove from heat and add rum.

Serves 2

Preparation time: 25 minutes

# NORTHERN SPY APPLE FRITTERS

$^3/_4$ cup yellow cornmeal

$^1/_2$ cup all-purpose flour

2 tablespoons baking powder

6 tablespoons sugar

pinch of salt

1 egg

$^1/_2$ cup milk

$1^1/_2$ cups vegetable oil (for frying)

1 Northern Spy apple, peeled, cored and chopped

2 tablespoons vegetable oil

confectioners' sugar (for garnish)

Makers 15 to 18 fritters

Preparation time: 40 minutes

Combine all dry ingredients (except confectioners' sugar). Add liquid ingredients (except $1^1/_2$ cups oil) one at a time, stirring between additions. Mix in apple. Let batter sit for 10 minutes. In a 1-quart saucepan over medium-high heat, heat the oil until it crackles, not quite to smoking point. Take precautionary measures for using hot oil!

Drop batter into the oil 1 tablespoon at a time (get close so the oil doesn't splash). Fry only 2 or 3 fritters at a time don't crowd the pan. Flip the fritters over and remove onto a paper towel when golden brown. Sprinkle with confectioners' sugar and serve.

# BANANA MUFFINS WITH DRIED APPLES AND APRICOTS

$^1$/$_2$ cup all-purpose flour

$^1$/$_2$ cup whole wheat flour

2 tablespoons baking powder

$^1$/$_4$ cup sugar

1 egg

2 tablespoons unsalted butter, melted and cooled

$^1$/$_2$ cup warm milk

1 banana, sliced

$^1$/$_4$ cup chopped dried apples

$^1$/$_4$ cup chopped dried apricots

pinch of salt

1 teaspoon vanilla extract

Preheat oven to 350ºF.

Combine flours, baking powder and sugar. Add egg, butter and milk, and mix. Stir in the banana, apples and apricots. Add salt and vanilla.

Fill 4 cups of a nonstick muffin pan (or regular muffin pan with paper liners) with the batter.

Bake for 8 to 10 minutes, until a toothpick inserted in the center comes out clean.

Serves 4

Preparation time: 20 minutes

# APPLE-HAZELNUT MUFFINS

$^1$/$_2$ cup hazelnuts, ground in blender to a coarse flour

$^1$/$_2$ cup all-purpose flour

2 tablespoons baking powder

$^1$/$_4$ cup sugar

1 egg

2 tablespoons unsalted butter, melted and cooled

$^1$/$_2$ cup warm milk

1 teaspoon vanilla extract

pinch of salt

$^1$/$_2$ cup chopped dried apples

Preheat oven to 350ºF.

Combine hazelnuts, flour, baking powder and sugar. Add egg, butter, milk, vanilla, salt and apples. Let stand 10 minutes.

Fill 4 cups of a nonstick muffin pan (or regular muffin pan with paper liners) with the batter.

Bake 8 to 10 minutes, until a toothpick inserted in the center comes out clean.

Serves 4

Preparation time: 30 minutes

# MACINTOSH APPLE
# AND SAUSAGE PIE

4 tablespoons cold unsalted butter, cut into small pieces

$^1/_2$ cup all-purpose flour

$^1/_2$ pound sweet sausage

1 tablespoon butter

1 MacIntosh apple, peeled, cored and diced

2 egg yolks

1 whole egg

1 cup heavy cream

salt

$^1/_2$ cup shredded sharp cheddar cheese

Serves 4 to 6

Preparation time: 1 hour 45 minutes

Preheat oven to 350ºF.

Combine 4 tablespoons cold butter with the flour and a pinch of salt. Mix with fingertips until butter is almost entirely incorporated and mixture has the consistency of coarse bread crumbs. Add 1 to 2 tablespoons cold water to bind. Refrigerate for 30 minutes.

Remove the sausage from its casing and crumble. In a skillet over medium-high heat, sauté the sausage until cooked through. Drain well. Set aside.

In a separate skillet, heat 1 tablespoon butter and sauté the apple for a minute, just until softened. Set aside.

Combine egg yolks and egg with cream and a pinch of salt. Set aside.

Roll out dough and press into a 9-inch pie tin. Place sausage in bottom of pie tin. Arrange apple on top of sausage and distribute cheese evenly over apple. Pour egg mixture over all. Bake for 50 minutes to 1 hour, until pie is somewhat firm when touched. Cool for a few minutes and serve warm.

# WINESAP APPLE TURNOVERS

3 tablespoons butter

2 Winesap apples, peeled, cored and diced

4 6-inch circles frozen puff pastry, thawed

1 egg, beaten with a little water

Serves 4

Preparation time: 25 minutes

Preheat oven to 350°F.

Melt 2 tablespoons butter in a skillet and sauté apples for a minute, just until softened. Cool. Grease a cookie sheet with remaining butter.

Arrange the apples in the center of the 4 pastry circles. Fold the circles in half and pinch the edges closed with your fingertips or a fork.

Brush the egg sparingly on the tops of the turnovers. Place on greased cookie sheet and bake for 8 to 10 minutes until the pastry has risen and is golden brown. Serve warm.

# SPICED MACOUN APPLE BREAD WITH WALNUTS

2 tablespoons butter

1 Macoun apple, peeled, cored and diced

$^1/_4$ cup walnuts, chopped

6 eggs, separated

6 tablespoons sugar

2 cups whole wheat flour, sifted

$^1/_2$ teaspoon nutmeg

$^1/_2$ teaspoon cinnamon

Preheat oven to 350ºF.

Melt 1 tablespoon butter in a skillet, and sauté apple and walnuts until apple is softened. Set aside to cool.

Beat egg whites until stiff. Combine sugar and egg yolks. Gradually fold beaten egg whites into yolks. Fold in flour. Add apples, walnuts and spices, being careful not to overmix or batter will deflate.

With remaining butter, grease a 8 x 4 x 3-inch loaf pan. Gently pour batter into pan and bake for 30 to 40 minutes, until a toothpick inserted in the center comes out clean.

Serves 6 to 8

Preparation time: 1 hour 15 minutes

# TWO
## SOUPS, SALADS AND APPETIZERS

# NORTHERN SPY APPLE AND BUTTERNUT SQUASH SOUP

VEGETABLE STOCK:

2 tablespoons vegetable oil

3 carrots, finely chopped

3-4 celery stalks, finely chopped

1 large Spanish onion, finely chopped

1 tablespoon whole black peppercorns

3-4 bay leaves

1 bunch parsley

SOUP:

2-3 Northern Spy apples, peeled, cored and coarsely chopped

1 butternut squash, peeled, seeded and coarsely chopped

salt

Serves 6

Preparation time: 2 hours 15 minutes

To make vegetable stock, heat oil in a 4-quart pot over medium heat. When hot, add vegetables, peppercorns, bay leaves and parsley. Sauté until vegetables are softened and begin to brown (about 20 minutes), being careful not to burn them. Add $2^1/2$ quarts cold water. Raise heat to high. Bring to a full boil, and then lower to a simmer. Cook for about 45 minutes, until stock is rich and flavorful. Strain and discard vegetables.

To make soup, return $1^1/2$ quarts strained stock to a simmer. Add the apples and the squash. Cook until tender, about 45 minutes.

Mash squash with a potato masher or force through a strainer if smooth purée is desired. Season with salt to taste. Add water if too thick; simmer longer if too thin.

# MACINTOSH APPLE AND BLUE CHEESE BISQUE

1 tablespoon unsalted butter

2 MacIntosh apples, peeled, cored and coarsely chopped

1¹/₂ cups milk

5-6 ounces blue cheese

salt and pepper

In a 2-quart saucepan over medium heat, melt the butter and sauté the apples until very soft.

Add the milk and lower the heat. When the milk starts to scald around the edges begin adding the cheese, bit by bit, stirring constantly. (The milk may begin to separate at this point; just keep adding the cheese and stirring.)

When all the cheese has been incorporated, add salt and pepper to taste.

Serves 2

Preparation time: 30 minutes

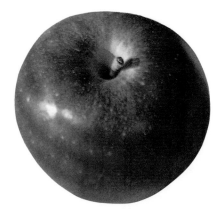

# GRANNY SMITH APPLE-ONION SOUP WITH CELERIAC

2 medium onions, coarsely chopped

2 large red potatoes, diced (skin optional)

3 Granny Smith apples, peeled, cored and chopped

1 medium celery root, peeled and diced

2 tablespoons vegetable oil

1 gallon chicken stock

salt and pepper

chopped chives for garnish (optional)

Serves 10

Preparation time: 1 hour 15 minutes

In a large pot, sauté onions, potatoes, apples and celery root in the oil.

When the onions are soft, add the chicken stock. Bring to a boil, then lower to a simmer and cook for about 40 minutes, until all the vegetables are very soft. Force through a sieve or purée in a blender. Return to pot and reheat. Add salt and pepper to taste. Serve garnished with chopped chives if desired.

# RADICCHIO, CHICORY AND GOLDEN DELICIOUS APPLE SALAD

1 head radicchio, leaves separated

2 heads Belgian endive, chopped

1 Golden Delicious apple, peeled, cored and diced

$^{1}/_{4}$ cup sour cream

Arrange radicchio on 4 plates.

Toss endive and apple together, and distribute evenly on the radicchio. Place a dollop of sour cream in the center of each salad.

Serves 4

Preparation time: 10 minutes

# WILTED GREENS WITH RED DELICIOUS APPLES AND BACON

1 bunch watercress

1 bunch dandelion greens

1 small red onion, sliced very thin

1 Red Delicious apple, peeled, cored and sliced thin

6 ounces bacon, cooked crisp, drained well and coarsely crumbled

1 lemon

In a 2-quart saucepan bring 2 cups water to a boil. Fit a strainer or colander on top of the pan, over but not in the water. Toss watercress and dandelion greens together in the strainer; cover and steam for about 2 to 3 minutes, checking frequently so the greens don't overcook.

When greens are just wilted, arrange on 4 plates.

Arrange onion slices on greens, and top with apple slices and crumbled bacon.

Squeeze lemon juice over each salad.

Serves 4

Preparation time: 15 minutes

# CRACKED WHEAT SALAD WITH JONATHAN APPLES AND MINT

$^3/_4$ cup cracked wheat (bulgur)

$^3/_4$ cup shelled pecans

2 Jonathan apples, peeled, cored and diced

2-3 plum tomatoes, seeded and diced

1 large sprig fresh mint, finely chopped

salt and pepper

1 tablespoon extra virgin olive oil

juice of 1 lemon

Soak cracked wheat in $^3/_4$ cup hot water for 30 minutes or until tender. Drain off any excess water.

Preheat oven to 350ºF.

While wheat is soaking, place the pecans in an ovenproof skillet and toast for about 5 minutes, until dark brown and aromatic. Cool. Combine nuts, wheat, apples, tomatoes and mint and season generously with salt and pepper. Sprinkle with olive oil and lemon juice.

Serves 2

Preparation time: 40 minutes

# SMOKED TURKEY AND GRAVENSTEIN APPLE SALAD

VINAIGRETTE:

2 tablespoons cider vinegar

6 tablespoons olive oil

1 tablespoon Dijon mustard

salt and pepper

SALAD:

1  bunch watercress

1  carrot, peeled and finely julienned

16 cherry tomatoes

10  ounces smoked turkey, coarsely chopped

2  cups vegetable oil

4  Gravenstein apples, peeled, cored and quartered

Serves 4

Preparation time: 25 minutes

Whisk together cider vinegar, olive oil and mustard, and add salt and pepper to taste. Refrigerate until needed.

Arrange watercress, carrot, tomatoes and turkey on 4 salad plates.

Heat the vegetable oil in a heavy, 1-quart skillet. When hot (about 350ºF), fry the apples until golden brown. Remove from oil and place on paper towels to drain. Arrange on the plates. Serve with the vinaigrette.

# ROME APPLE AND GOAT'S CHEESE TARTLETS

$^1/_2$ cup cold unsalted butter, cut into small pieces

1 cup all-purpose flour

pinch of salt

1 Rome apple, peeled, cored and thinly sliced

$^1/_2$ pound goat cheese

Preheat oven to 350ºF.

Combine butter, flour and salt with fingertips until butter is mostly incorporated and the mixture has the consistency of coarse bread crumbs. Add 2 to 3 tablespoons cold water to bind. Refrigerate for 30 minutes. Roll out and press into eight 2-inch tart shells. (Excess dough can be wrapped and refrigerated for up to 2 weeks.)

Arrange 2 or 3 slices of apple in each tart shell. Place shells on a cookie sheet and bake for about 20 minutes, until crusts are golden brown. Let stand until cool enough to handle.

Place 1 ounce of cheese in each tart and bake 5 minutes, until cheese softens and begins to brown. Serve warm.

Makes 8 tartlets

Preparation time: 1 hour 15 minutes

# GREENING APPLE AND SPINACH PÂTÉ

2 Greening apples, peeled, cored and coarsely chopped

2-3 tablespoons unsalted butter

1 pound fresh spinach, washed thoroughly and stems removed

2 eggs

1¼ cups walnuts, ground in blender to a coarse flour

¾ cup fresh unseasoned bread

crumbs

salt and pepper

Serves 4 to 6

Preparation time: 2 hours 15 minutes, set overnight

Sauté apples in butter until soft. Remove apples and set aside. Sauté spinach in remaining butter until wilted and drain well. Purée in blender or food processor.

Beat together eggs, walnuts, spinach, apples and bread crumbs. Add salt and pepper to taste.

Lay a large piece of plastic wrap on a table or counter and pour the mixture lengthwise down the center of the plastic. Roll the plastic around the mixture to form a log, approximately 3 inches in diameter. Tie the ends closed with string and refrigerate for at least 1 hour. When thoroughly chilled, remove pâté from the refrigerator and reshape log (leaving it wrapped); it should be as smooth and cylindrical as possible.

Fill a large skillet or shallow saucepan with enough water to cover the pâté and place over medium heat. Bring to a simmer and reduce heat so water is just barely moving. Place the pâté in the water and poach for 30 to 45 minutes, until firm.

Remove from water and refrigerate overnight. Peel off plastic wrap and slice to serve.

# THREE

## MAIN

## COURSES

# BAKED CORTLAND APPLES WITH YAM FILLING

1 tablespoon vegetable oil

1 yam, peeled and diced

1  small red bell pepper, diced

1 medium onion, diced

$1/4$ teaspoon fresh chopped or dried thyme

salt and pepper

2 slices firm white bread, crumbled

1 14-ounce can whole peeled tomatoes

4 Cortland apples, cored and hollowed out

Preheat oven to 400ºF.

Heat oil over medium heat and sauté yam, pepper and onion with thyme until soft. Add salt and pepper to taste. Set aside.

Combine pepper and onion mixture with bread and 3 or 4 tablespoons of juice from the can of tomatoes.

Stuff mixture into the apples. Place the tomatoes and remaining juice into an ovenproof, non-reactive skillet and arrange the apples on top. Bake for 25 to 30 minutes, until apples are tender.

Serves 4

Preparation time: 1 hour

# GRILLED SWORDFISH WITH LADY APPLE BUTTER

$^1/_4$ cup unsalted butter, softened

1 Lady apple, peeled, cored and finely chopped

salt and pepper

2 7-8-ounce pieces of swordfish

2 tablespoons olive or vegetable oil

Serves 2

Preparation time: 30 minutes

Preheat grill to high following manufacturer's instructions. (Or use a broiler if a grill is unavailable.)  Using a small piece of the butter in a skillet, sauté the apple until tender.

Combine the softened butter, cooked apple and salt and pepper to taste. Roll into a log in foil, plastic wrap or the butter wrapper, and refrigerate until hardened.

Rub the swordfish with the oil and some salt and pepper. Place on the hottest spot on the grill (or under the broiler). Cook for about 3 to 4 minutes; turn 90 degrees with a spatula, and cook for another 3 to 4 minutes. Flip swordfish over onto a cooler spot on the grill, and cook for another 3 to 4 minutes.

Place the fish on 2 plates and slice the cold butter onto the fish.

# BROOK TROUT BAKED IN PARCHMENT WITH NORTHERN SPY APPLES

2 whole brook trout, cleaned, heads and fins removed

2 pieces parchment paper cut into 12-inch circles

4 slices lemon

4 sprigs fresh or 1 teaspoon dried thyme

1 Northern Spy apple, peeled, cored, quartered and sliced

2-3 scallions, chopped

2 tablespoons unsalted butter

salt and pepper

Preheat oven to 400°F.

Place each trout, opened, in the center of each piece of parchment paper.

Place 2 slices of lemon, 2 sprigs of fresh thyme (or $\frac{1}{2}$ teaspoon dried thyme), half of the sliced apple, half of the chopped scallions and 1 tablespoon butter inside each trout. Add salt and pepper to taste.

Close up trouts. Fold paper in half over fish to form a semicircle, and make small overlapping folds along the rim to seal.

Place fish in paper in an 11- x 14-inch baking pan, and bake for 20 minutes. Serve inside paper.

Serves 2

Preparation time: 35 minutes

# BARBECUED PRAWNS WITH JONATHAN APPLE AND QUINCE CHUTNEY

CHUTNEY:

$^1/_4$ cup sugar

$^1/_2$ cup dried apricots, chopped

5-6 pitted prunes, chopped

$^1/_4$ cup golden raisins

2 Jonathan apples, peeled, cored and coarsely chopped

$^1/_4$ cup quince preserves

$^1/_4$ cup bourbon

SHRIMP:

12 medium-sized shrimp, peeled and deveined

Serves 2

(Makes 375-500 ml [12-16 fl oz] chutney)

Preparation time: 45 minutes

In a heavy skillet dissolve sugar in 1 cup water over medium heat. Add apricots, prunes and raisins, and cook for 4 to 5 minutes.

Add apples and preserves. Cook until apples are tender. Remove from heat and add bourbon. Cool.

Preheat grill to high following manufacturer's instructions. (May be broiled if a grill is unavailable.)

Skewer shrimp. Brush chutney (including the chunks of fruit) generously on all sides of shrimp and place on the hottest spot on the grill (or under the broiler). Turn occasionally, brushing the shrimp with more chutney. Cook until shrimp are firm to the touch, about 6 minutes. Store extra chutney in a glass jar in the refrigerator for up to 4 weeks.

# RED SNAPPER WITH EMPIRE APPLES AND WALNUTS

$^1$/$_4$ cup walnut pieces

2  7-8-ounce red snapper fillets

salt and pepper

$^1$/$_4$ cup all-purpose flour

3  tablespoons vegetable oil

2  Empire apples, peeled, cored and chopped

2-3 leaves fresh sage, chopped, or $^1$/$_2$ teaspoon dried sage

(optional)

Serves 2

Preparation time: 20 minutes

Preheat oven to 400ºF.

Place the walnuts in an ovenproof skillet and toast in the oven for about 5 minutes, until darkened a shade and aromatic. Remove from oven, cool and set aside.

Lightly dust the fish with salt, pepper and flour.

Place an ovenproof skillet with 2 tablespoons oil over medium-high heat. When oil is hot, place the fish, flesh side down, in the pan. Lower the heat.

When the fish is golden brown, turn it over and place it in the oven for about 5 to 6 minutes.

In a separate skillet, heat the remaining tablespoon of oil. Add apples, toasted walnuts, sage (if desired) and salt and pepper. Sauté for a few minutes until the apples are tender.

Remove fish from the oven and place on 2 plates. Spoon apples and nuts onto the fish.

# TURKEY POTPIE WITH NEWTOWN PIPPINS AND ONIONS

2 cups all-purpose flour

1 cup unsalted butter, cut into small pieces

pinch of salt

2 tablespoons vegetable oil

1 large Spanish onion, chopped

$^1/_4$ pound cooked turkey, coarsely chopped

$^1/_4$ cup white wine

$^1/_4$ cup heavy cream

$^1/_4$ cup yellow cornmeal

2 sprigs fresh mint, chopped (optional)

salt and pepper

2 Newtown Pippins, peeled, cored and chopped

1 egg, beaten

Preheat oven to 350ºF.

In a bowl, combine flour, butter and a pinch of salt. Mix together with fingertips until butter is mostly incorporated and mixture has the consistency of coarse bread crumbs. Add 4 to 5 tablespoons cold water to bind. Form into a patty and refrigerate for 30 minutes. While dough chills, make the filling. Heat the vegetable oil in a large skillet over medium hear.

Add the onion and cook until soft. Add the turkey. Cook for 2 to 3 minutes until turkey softens. Add wine and reduce for 2 to 3 minutes. Add cream.

Bring to a boil and reduce 2 to 3 minutes. Add cornmeal, mint (if desired), salt, pepper and apples. Cook for another 5 minutes.

Fill 4 individual 5-inch round casserole dishes with the filling. Roll out dough and cut into the shape of the dishes. Place on top of the turkey filling, and brush with the beaten egg.

Bake for 30 to 40 minutes until crust is golden brown.

Serves 4

Preparation time: 1 hour 30 minutes

# DUCK BREASTS WITH CRAB APPLES

1-2 tablespoons vegetable oil

2 boneless duck breasts, trimmed of fat

2 tablespoons all-purpose flour

4 Crab Apples, quartered and cored

1-2 sprigs fresh thyme

salt and pepper

Serves 2

Preparation time: 15 minutes

Preheat oven to 400ºF.

In an ovenproof skillet, heat the oil to smoking point. Dust the breasts lightly with flour and place in the hot skillet skin side down. Cook for 1 to 2 minutes until golden brown; turn over; reduce heat and add the apple quarters and thyme. Sprinkle salt, pepper and 2 to 3 tablespoons water over all ingredients.

Place the skillet in the oven for 5 to 6 minutes. Duck breasts should be somewhat firm (medium rare to medium) and apples should be soft and wilted.

Slice breasts and arrange on plates with apples, thyme and remaining juices from the pan.

# CHICKEN AND CORTLAND APPLE COUSCOUS

2 cups coarsely chopped cooked chicken

2 cups dry couscous

2$^1$/$_2$ cups boiling chicken stock

$^1$/$_2$ cup golden raisins

$^1$/$_2$ cup toasted slivered almonds

2 Cortland apples, peeled, cored and coarsely chopped

$^1$/$_4$ cup unsalted butter, cut into small pieces

$^1$/$_2$ teaspoon ground coriander seeds

$^1$/$_4$ teaspoon ground cinnamon

$^1$/$_8$ teaspoon ground cloves

Preheat oven to 400°F.

Combine all ingredients in a 9 x 13 x 2-inch glass baking pan. Cover with foil and bake for 25 minutes.

Serves 4

Preparation time: 45 minutes

# PORK CHOPS WITH ROME APPLE AND ROSEMARY STUFFING

2 leeks, white part only, split lengthwise, washed and chopped, or 1 medium Spanish onion, finely diced

1/4 cup vegetable oil

1 medium-sized Idaho potato, grated, with skin

1 sprig fresh rosemary, leaves removed and finely chopped, or 1/2 teaspoon dried rosemary

1 Rome apple, peeled, cored and diced

1 slice firm white or whole wheat bread, crumbled

salt and pepper

8 pork chops (preferably loin chops)

In a large frying pan, sauté the leeks in half of the vegetable oil until soft. Add the potato and rosemary.

Add the apple and continue frying. You may need to add some water if the mixture is too dry. When the potato is tender, add the bread and salt and pepper to taste. Lower heat to keep the stuffing warm. In a separate frying pan (you may need 2 for all 8 chops), sauté the pork chops in remaining oil for 6 to 8 minutes per side, making sure the oil is hot before you add the chops. Serve with a spoonful of the stuffing.

Serves 4

Preparation time: 35 minutes

# SPARERIBS WITH APPLESAUCE GLAZE

2 racks pork spareribs, skin removed from bone side

salt and pepper

1¼ cups applesauce

Serves 4 to 6

Preparation time: 2 hours 30 minutes, plus cooling time, plus 15 minutes. (It is best to begin this recipe the day before or at least 6 hours prior to serving.)

Preheat oven to 350°F.

Season ribs generously with salt and pepper on both sides.

Place ribs, standing up on their sides, in an ovenproof skillet. Add 1 cup of water. Cover with aluminum foil and bake for 2 to 2½ hours. Remove carefully from oven and let cool at least 2 hours or overnight.

When the ribs are cooled, cut into individual pieces.

Preheat grill to high following manufacturer's instructions. (May be broiled if a grill is unavailable.)

Brush ribs with applesauce and place on the grill (or under the broiler). Turn ribs, continuing to apply applesauce with a brush, until meat is tender and heated throughout, about 10 minutes.

# GRILLED VEAL CHOPS AND GRANNY SMITH APPLES

2 10-ounce veal chops

2 tablespoons vegetable oil

salt and pepper

2 tablespoons unsalted butter, softened

2 Granny Smith apples, sliced crosswise into 1/2-inch rounds

(do not peel or core)

Serves 2

Preparation time: 20 minutes

Preheat grill to high following manufacturer's instructions. (Or use a broiler if a grill is unavailable.)

Rub veal chops with vegetable oil and season with salt and pepper. Place on the hottest spot on the grill (or under the broiler).

Rub softened butter on apple slices and sprinkle with salt and pepper. Place on the coolest spot on the grill (or under the broiler).

Turn veal chops every few minutes until they are firm to the touch, about 10 minutes.

Turn apple slices until golden brown on both sides and tender. Veal chops and apples should be ready at about the same time if they are begun together.

# FOUR
## ACCOMPANIMENTS

# BRAISED RED CABBAGE WITH NORTHERN SPY APPLES

2 tablespoons vegetable oil

2 small red onions, peeled, halved and sliced

1 small head red cabbage, outer leaves removed, quartered and sliced

2 Northern Spy apples, peeled, cored and julienned

2 tablespoons caraway seeds

2 cups dry vermouth

salt and pepper

Heat the oil in a large skillet. Add the onions and cabbage and sauté for a few seconds. Add the apples and caraway seeds. Toss ingredients together.

Remove from heat; add the vermouth and return to heat. Bring to a simmer; cover and cook for about 6 to 7 minutes until cabbage is tender but still a bit crunchy. Add salt and pepper to taste.

Serves 8

Preparation time: 30 minutes

# CARAMELIZED GREENING APPLES AND PEARL ONIONS

2 tablespoons unsalted butter

1 cup fresh pearl onions, peeled

salt and pepper

2 Greening apples, peeled, cored and quartered

In a heavy skillet over medium heat, melt butter and sauté onions until translucent. Add salt and pepper to taste.

Cut each apple quarter in half crosswise and add to the pan. Cook, tossing occasionally, until golden brown. Lower heat if necessary.

Serves 4 to 6

Preparation time: 30 minutes

# FRESH GOLDEN DELICIOUS APPLE-WALNUT RELISH

1 cup shelled walnuts

2 Golden Delicious apples, peeled, cored and diced

$^1/_2$ cup sweet red wine

Preheat oven to 350ºF.

Place walnuts in a pan and toast for 5 minutes until dark brown and aromatic. Cool and chop.

Combine all ingredients. Best when served the next day.

Serves 6 to 8

Preparation time: 15 minutes

# GINGERED CRAB APPLE SAUCE

3 pounds Crab Apples, stems removed

1 4-6 ounce piece fresh ginger, peeled and coarsely chopped, or 2-3 tablespoons ground ginger

2 cups cranberry juice

Place the apples in a heavy-bottomed, 6-quart pot (copper is best.)

Add the fresh ginger. If you are using ground ginger, wait until the end to add it.

Add cranberry juice.

Cook on low heat for 45 minutes to 1 hour, stirring frequently. You may need to add a little water.

When the apples are cooked through and very soft, force the"meat" through a sieve or stainless steel strainer into a bowl. Add ground ginger now if using. (Taste the applesauce as you add the ginger, as the intensity of dried spices can vary widely depending on their age, the brand, even the light and heat conditions under which they are stored.) Allow to cool. Serve warm or cold.

Serves 15

Preparation time: 1 hour 15 minutes

# CARROT, PARSNIP AND GRANNY SMITH APPLE COLESLAW

4 carrots, shredded

3 small parsnips, shredded

2 Granny Smith apples, peeled, cored and finely chopped

$^1/_4$ head red cabbage, shredded

1 small red onion, thinly sliced (optional)

2 tablespoons chopped parsley

$^1/_2$ cup mayonnaise

1 tablespoon sugar

salt and pepper

Combine carrots, parsnips, apples, cabbage, onion and parsley.

Add mayonnaise, sugar, and salt and pepper to taste. Mix all ingredients well.

Serves 6 to 8

Preparation time: 45 minutes

# THREE-APPLE APPLE BUTTER

1 pound unsalted butter

1 Granny Smith apple, quartered (with core and skin)

1 Winesap apple, quartered (with core and skin)

1 Macoun apple, quartered (with core and skin)

Place all ingredients in a heavy, 4-quart saucepan and cook over medium-low to medium heat.

Simmer for about 30 minutes, lowering the heat as the apples cook and stirring occasionally.

Force through a sieve or stainless steel strainer. Cool thoroughly and refrigerate, covered.

Makes 750 ml (1¼ pints)

Preparation time: 45 minutes

# FIVE
## DESSERTS

# CRAN-APPLE PIE

CRUST:

$^1/_2$ cup cold unsalted butter, cut into small pieces

1 cup all-purpose flour

2 tablespoons sugar

pinch of salt

TOPPING:

$^1/_4$ cup cold unsalted butter, cut into small pieces

$^1/_2$ cup all-purpose flour

$^1/_2$ cup light brown sugar

FILLING:

$^1/_4$ cup fresh or frozen cranberries

4-5 Red Delicious apples, peeled, cored and coarsely chopped

$^1/_4$ cup sugar

pinch of salt

Preheat oven to 350ºF.

Combine crust ingredients in a bowl and mix together with your fingertips, breaking up butter until mixture has the consistency of coarse bread crumbs. Add 2 to 3 tablespoons cold water to bind, and form into a patty. Refrigerate for 30 minutes.

Combine butter and flour for topping with fingertips, breaking butter into small, pea-sized pieces. Stir in brown sugar, allowing some lumps to remain. Set aside.

Combine filling ingredients and set aside.

Roll dough out into a circle and press into a 9-inch pie tin.

Fill pastry-lined tin with apple-cranberry mixture and sprinkle topping over all.

Bake 50 minutes to 1 hour, until pastry is golden brown. Let cool before serving.

Serves 6

Preparation time: 1 hour 45 minutes

# CALVADOS SOUFFLÉ

1 tablespoon unsalted butter

1 Golden Delicious apple, peeled, cored and finely chopped

pinch of salt

4 eggs, separated

$^1/_2$ cup sugar

$^1/_4$ cup calvados

Serves 4

Preparation time: 45 minutes

Preheat oven to 350°F.

Grease four 6-ounce soufflé cups with butter and refrigerate.

Toss apple with salt in a large bowl. Set aside until juices form at the bottom of the bowl.

Combine egg yolks, sugar and calvados and set aside.

Whisk egg whites in a dry bowl until stiff peaks form.

Add a little of the beaten egg white to the yolk mixture, then a bit more. Very gently fold the entire yolk mixture into the remaining whites until completely incorporated. Carefully fold in the apple and its juices.

Pour batter into the buttered soufflé cups.

Place the soufflé cups in a 2-inch-deep baking tray filled with enough water to immerse the cups about $^3/_4$ of the way to their tops. Bake for about 12 to 15 minutes, until tops have risen about half an inch above the rims of the cups. It might take a few tries to know exactly when to take the soufflés out of the oven – don't overcook!

# JONATHAN APPLES POACHED IN RED WINE

4 Jonathan apples

1$^1$/$_2$ cups flavorful red wine such as Bordeaux or Burgundy

2 teaspoons honey

Serves 4

Preparation time: 30 minutes

Peel the apples, leaving a little skin at the top. With a small spoon, scoop out the core from the bottom. This will allow the apples to poach evenly.

In a saucepan, heat the wine to a low simmer. Place the apples in the wine, skin side up. Cook for about 20 minutes. When a small knife or toothpick can be inserted easily, remove the apples.

If the wine is greatly reduced, add about 2 teaspoons of water along with the honey. Heat until the honey has dissolved. Again, if the sauce is too thick, add a little water; if it is too thin, allow to cook down more. Spoon the sauce over the apples.

# MACINTOSH APPLE CRUMBLE WITH VANILLA ICE CREAM

4 MacIntosh apples, peeled, cored and cut into large pieces

$^1/_4$ cup sugar

pinch of salt

$^1/_2$ cup cold unsalted butter, cut into small pieces

$^3/_4$ cup all-purpose flour

$^1/_2$ cup light brown sugar

1 pint vanilla ice cream

Serves 4

Preparation time: 45 minutes

Preheat oven to 350ºF.

Toss apples, sugar and salt together. Divide equally among 4 individual ovenproof bowls, ramekins or gratin dishes.

Combine butter and flour with fingertips until mixture is crumbly and has the texture of oatmeal. Add brown sugar, allowing lumps to remain in mixture. Distribute evenly over apples.

Bake 30 minutes. Serve warm or cold with a scoop of vanilla ice cream.

# WINESAP APPLE PUDDING

$^3/_4$ cup bourbon

1 cup sugar

$^1/_4$ teaspoon ground nutmeg

$^1/_2$ teaspoon ground cloves

2 teaspoons ground cinnamon

5 eggs

1 quart heavy cream

2 teaspoons unsalted butter

10 slices white bread, crusts trimmed

$^1/_2$ cup raisins

2 Winesap apples, peeled, cored and chopped

Serves 8

Preparation time: 1 hour 20 minutes, set overnight

Preheat oven to 350ºF.

Combine bourbon, sugar, spices, eggs and cream. Set aside.

Grease a 6-inch-deep loaf pan with the butter.

Arrange 2$^1/_2$ slices of bread on bottom of loaf pan. Cover with one third of the raisins and apple pieces. Arrange 2$^1/_2$ more slices; cover with more raisins and apples. Repeat a third time until all of the ingredients are used up. Don't place any raisins or apples on the top layer of bread.

Pour bourbon mixture over bread until it is all absorbed. Bake for about 1 hour, until firm. Cool overnight and serve cold or warm.

# CANDIED LADY APPLES

1¹/₂ cups sugar

6 Lady apples

Serves 6

Preparation time: 15 minutes

In a heavy saucepan, boil sugar and 4 tablespoons water for 3 to 4 minutes.

To test when sugar is ready, take a bit of boiling mixture and drop it into a glass of cold water. If the sugar forms a hard ball it's ready. If it forms a soft ball that you can mold with your fingers after being dropped in the water, cook for a few more minutes. (A candy thermometer should read 250°F.)

Make sure apples are thoroughly washed and dried. Poke a stick into each apple and dip apples into the hot sugar mixture. Place directly onto wax paper and let cool.

# GRANNY SMITH APPLE SORBET

6 Granny Smith apples, peeled and cored

²/₃ cup lemon juice, lime juice or a combination of both

¹/₂ cup sugar

¹/₂ cup calvados or applejack

Slice 5 of the apples and purée in a blender or food processor. Chop the sixth apple finely.

Combine all ingredients and whisk together until sugar is dissolved.

Pour into 1¹/₂-quart (or larger) electric or hand-operated ice cream maker. Process until firm following manufacturer's instructions.

Serve immediately or freeze for later use.

Serves 6

Preparation time: 30 minutes to 1 hour

# GOLDEN DELICIOUS APPLE AND CINNAMON ICE CREAM

2 Golden Delicious apples, peeled, cored and chopped

1 quart heavy cream

5 egg yolks

1 cup sugar

2 tablespoons vanilla extract

2 teaspoons ground cinnamon (or to taste)

Combine all ingredients in a bowl. Whisk together until smooth and sugar has dissolved.

Pour mixture into a 2-quart (or larger) electric or hand- operated ice cream maker. Process until firm following manufacturer's instructions.

Serve immediately or freeze for later use.

Serves 8

Preparation time: 30 minutes to 1 hour

# MACOUN APPLE PIE

CRUST:

1 cup cold unsalted butter, cut into small pieces

2 cups all-purpose flour

2 tablespoons sugar

pinch of salt

1 egg

FILLING:

5 Macoun apples, peeled, cored and thinly sliced

$^1/_4$ cup sugar (or less if you prefer)
pinch of salt

Serves 6

Preparation time: 1 hour 45 minutes

Preheat oven to 350ºF.

With your fingertips, combine butter, flour, sugar and salt until butter is almost entirely incorporated in the flour. Allow some butter pieces (the size of a lentil or smaller) to remain; this will promote flakiness when the pastry is baked. Add 4 to 5 tablespoons cold water to bind, and form dough into a patty. Refrigerate for 30 minutes.

Combine filling ingredients and set aside.

Roll out half of the dough using additional flour to dust the tabletop, and press into a 9-inch pie tin.

Fill the pastry-lined tin with the apple mixture, packing tightly.

Roll out the remaining dough and cut into $^3/_4$-inch-wide strips. Arrange strips in a crisscross pattern over the apples. When the entire pie is covered, trim and press the edges together.

Beat the egg with 2 tablespoons cold water. With a brush or fingertips spread the egg wash on the dough strips and on the edges.

Bake 50 minutes to 1 hour, until crust is golden brown.

Cool with a cloth on top to prevent the filling from retracting too far from the crust.

# GOLDEN DELICIOUS APPLES WITH CARAMEL AND COOKIES

COOKIES:

7 tablespoons unsalted butter, softened

6 tablespoons sugar

$^1/_4$ teaspoon vanilla extract

$^3/_4$ cup all-purpose flour

pinch of salt

CARAMEL:

$^1/_4$ cup sugar

$^1/_4$ cup heavy cream

$^1/_2$ cup unsalted butter, softened

APPLES:

2 Golden Delicious apples, cored

$^1/_4$ cup chopped pecans (optional)

Preheat oven to 350ºF.

To make cookie dough, combine 6 tablespoons butter with the sugar and vanilla until smooth. Add flour and salt. Mix until dough forms a ball. Roll into a log and refrigerate.

When the dough is firm cut into 8 equal slices.

Grease a cookie sheet with the remaining butter. Place the slices of dough on the cookie sheet and bake for 8 to 10 minutes until the edges turn brown. Cool.

To make caramel, cook the sugar and 2 tablespoons water in a heavy saucepan for about 8 to 10 minutes over medium heat, until golden brown and bubbly.

Lower heat and slowly add the heavy cream, stirring constantly with a whisk.

After all the cream is added cook for about 2 to 3 minutes. Remove from heat and stir in butter a little at a time.

Slice apples thinly and arrange over cookies on 4 plates.Pour hot caramel on top. Sprinkle with chopped nuts if desired.

Serves 4

Preparation time: 1 hour

# BAKED ROME APPLES WITH COINTREAU

2 Rome apples, peeled and cored

1-1½ cups Cointreau liqueur

Serves 2

Preparation time: 1 hour

Preheat oven to 350ºF.

Place the apples and the liqueur in an ovenproof skillet or saucepan.

Bake for 1 hour, basting every 10 to 15 minutes.

# JONATHAN APPLE DUMPLINGS

1 tablespoon butter

2 cups all-purpose flour

pinch of salt

3 tablespoons sugar

1 tablespoon baking powder

$^3/_4$ cup cold unsalted butter, cut into small pieces

$^1/_2$ cup buttermilk

3 Jonathan apples, peeled, cored and quartered

Serves 6

Preparation time: 1 hour

Preheat oven to 350ºF.

Grease a cookie sheet with the tablespoon of butter.

Combine flour, salt, 2 tablespoons sugar and the baking powder. Mix in cold butter with your fingertips. Add the buttermilk and work into a dough.

Roll out the dough and cut into 12 circles. Place an apple quarter on each piece of dough, fold the dough over the apples and pinch closed. Sprinkle remaining sugar over the dumplings. Place on greased cookie sheet and bake 35 to 40 minutes, until golden brown.

# EMPIRE APPLE AND PEAR TARTS

CRUST:

1½ cups all-purpose flour

¾ cup cold unsalted butter, cut into small pieces

1-2 tablespoons sugar

pinch of salt

FILLING:

½ pound almond paste

3 egg yolks

¼ cup sugar

½ cup unsalted butter, softened

TOPPING:

2 Empire apples, peeled, cored and thinly sliced

2 pears, peeled, cored and thinly sliced

½ cup raspberry jam mixed with a little water

Serves 4

Preparation time: 1 hour 13 minutes

Preheat oven to 350ºF.

Combine crust ingredients in bowl with fingertips until the consistency of coarse bread crumbs. Add 2 to 3 tablespoons cold water to bind. Form into a ball and refrigerate for 30 minutes.

Mix all filling ingredients in a blender or food processor.

Roll out dough and press into four 6-inch-round tart tins. Spread filling on the bottom of each. Arrange apple and pear slices on top of filling. Brush raspberry jam over tops evenly. Bake for 25 to 30 minutes. Cool.

# SIX
## BEVERAGES

# APPLE-APRICOT SMOOTHIE

1 Golden Delicious apple, peeled, cored and chopped

1 cup apple juice

4 fresh apricots, pitted (skin optional)

1 banana, peeled

$^3/_4$ cup plain yogurt

10-12 ice cubes

1 tablespoon honey

Place all ingredients in a blender and process until smooth.

Serves 2 to 4
Preparation time: 3 minutes

# APPLE-CRANBERRY ICED TEA

$^1/_2$ cup fresh or frozen cranberries

$^1/_4$ pound dried apples

1 cinnamon stick

3-4 whole cloves

Place the cranberries and 1 quart cold water in a 2-quart saucepan. Bring to a boil.

Place the apples, cinnamon stick and cloves in a 2-quart teapot and add the boiling water and cranberries.

Let steep for several minutes and strain. Let cool and serve over ice.

(Also delicious hot!)

Serves 4
Preparation time: 10 minutes

# HOT BUTTERED APPLE JUICE

4 teaspoons unsalted butter

3 ounces dark rum

2 cups apple cider

Place the butter at the bottom of 2 mugs. Add half of the rum to each.

In a small saucepan (or in the microwave) heat the cider until just scalded. Pour over the butter and rum.

Serves 2
Preparation time: 3 minutes

# APPLEJACK PUNCH

10-12  ice cubes

4 cups apple cider

1 cup ginger ale

2-3 whole cinnamon sticks

1 cup applejack

Combine all ingredients in a bowl or pitcher. Add the applejack last, a little at a time, tasting for desired potency.

Serves 6
Preparation time: 3 minutes

# CALVADOS SPRITZER

8-10 ice cubes

1 cup calvados

2 ounces sparkling water

Place the ice cubes in 2 tall glasses. Pour the calvados equally into the glasses. Add 1 ounce sparkling water to each, or adjust amount for desired potency.

Serves 2

Preparation time: 1 minute

# APPLE JUICE SPRITZER

8-10 ice cubes

1$^1$/$_2$ cups apple cider

2 ounces sparkling water

Place the ice cubes in 2 tall cocktail glasses. Pour the cider equally into the glasses. Add 1 ounce sparkling water to each, or adjust amount to taste.

Serves 2

Preparation time: 1 minute

# RECIPE LIST

Greening Appleand Spinach Pâté
50

Grilled Swordfish with Lady Apple Butter
56

Grilled Veal Chops and Granny Smith
Apples
74

Hot Buttered Cider
118

Jonathan Apple Dumplings
110

Jonathan Apples Poached in Red Wine
92

MacIntosh Apple and Blue Cheese Bisque
36

Mac1ntosh Apple and Sausage Pie
26

MacIntosh Apple Cobblers with Vanilla Ice
Cream
94

Macoun Apple Pie
104

Northern Spy Apple and Butternut Squash
Soup
34

Northern Spy Apple Fritters
22

Oatmeal Pancakes with Jonathan Apples and
Pecans
18

Pork Chops with Rome Apple and
Rosemary Stuffing
70

Radicchio, Endive and Golden Delicious
Apple Salad
40

Red Snapper with Empire Apples and
Walnuts
62

Rome Apple and Goat Cheese Tartlets
48

Rome Apple, Orange and Prune Compote
20

Smoked Turkey and Gravenstein Apple
Salad
46

Spareribs with Applesauce Glaze
72

Spiced Macoun Apple Bread with Walnuts
30

Three-Apple Apple Butter
84

Turkey Potpie with Newtown Pippins and
Onions
64

Wilted Greens with Red Delicious Apples
and Bacon
42

Winesap Apple Pudding
96

Winesap Apple Turnovers
32

# RECIPE LIST BY APPLE OR APPLE PRODUCT

APPLEJACK

Applejack Punch
118

APPLESAUCE

Spareribs with Applesauce Glaze
72

CALVADOS

Calvados Soufflé
90

Calvados Spritzer
120

CIDER

Apple Cider Spritzer
120

Applejack Punch
118

Hot Buttered Cider
118

CORTLAND

Baked Cortland Apples with Yam Filling
54

Chicken and Cortland Apple Couscous
68

CRAB APPLES

Duck Breasts with Crab Apples
66

Ginger Crab Apple Applesauce
80

DRIED APPLES

Apple-Cranberry Iced Tea
116

Apple-Hazelnut Muffins
24

Banana Muffins with Dried Apples and
Apricots
24

## Empire

Empire Apple and Pear Tarts
112

Red Snapper with Empire Apples and
Walnuts
62

## Golden Delicious

Apple-Apricot Smoothie
116

Fresh Golden Delicious Apple-Walnut
Relish
80

Golden Delicious Apple and Cinnamon Ice
Cream
102

Golden Delicious Apples with Caramel and
Cookies
106

Radicchio, Endive and Golden Delicious
Apple Salad
40

## Granny Smith

Carrot, Parsnip and Granny Smith Apple
Coleslaw
82

Granny Smith Apple-Onion Soup with
Celery Root
38

Granny Smith Apple Sorbet
100

Grilled Veal Chops and Granny Smith
Apples
74

Three-Apple Apple Butter
84

## Gravenstein

Smoked Turkey and Gravenstein Apple
Salad
46

## Greening

Caramelized Greening Apples and Pearl
Onions
78

Greening Apple and Spinach Pâté
50

## JONATHAN

Barbecued Shrimp with Jonathan Apple and
Quince Chutney
60

Cracked Wheat Salad with Jonathan Apples
and Mint
44

Jonathan Apple Dumplings
110

Jonathan Apples Poached in Red Wine
92

Oatmeal Pancakes with Jonathan Apples and
Pecans
18

## JUICE

Apple-Apricot Smoothie
116

## LADY APPLES

Candied Lady Apples
98

Grilled Swordfish with Lady Apple Butter
56

## MACOUN

Macoun Apple Pie
104

Spiced Macoun Apple Bread with Walnuts
30

Three-Apple Apple Butter
84

## MACINTOSH

Macintosh Apple and Blue Cheese Bisque
36

Macintosh Apple and Sausage Pie
26

Macintosh Apple Cobblers with Vanilla ice
Cream
94

## NEWTOWN PIPPINS

Turkey Potpie with Newtown Pippins and
Onions
64

## Northern Spy

Braised Red Cabbage with Northern Spy
Apples
78

Brook Trout Baked in Parchment with
Northern Spy Apples
58

Northern Spy Apple and Butternut Squash
Soup
34

Northern Spy Apple Fritters
22

## Red Delicious

Cran-Apple Pie
88

Wilted Greens with Red Delicious Apples
and Bacon
42

## Rome

Baked Rome Apples with Cointreau
108

Pork Chops with Rome Apple and
Rosemary Stuffing
72

Rome Apple and Goat Cheese Tartlets
48

Rome Apple, Orange and Prune Compote
20

## Winesap

Three-Apple Apple Butter
84

Winesap Apple Pudding
96

Winesap Apple Turnovers
28

BERRIES
*A Cookbook*

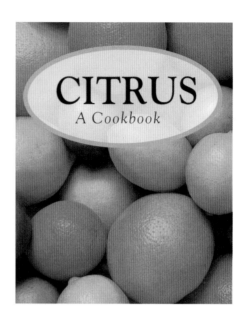

CITRUS
*A Cookbook*

NUTS
*A Cookbook*

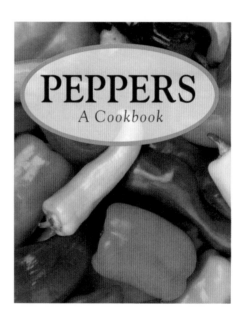

PEPPERS
*A Cookbook*